Sorry I Don't Have the Time
Poems about Modern Life

Collected Poems by
Micheline Mason
1973 - 2011

Order this book online at www.trafford.com
or email orders@trafford.com

Most Trafford titles are also available at major online book retailers.

Printed in the United States of America.

ISBN: 978-1-4269-6259-2 (sc)
ISBN: 978-1-4269-6261-5 (hc)
ISBN: 978-1-4269-6262-2 (e)

Library of Congress Control Number: 2011905562

Trafford rev. 04/06/2011

Trafford
PUBLISHING www.trafford.com

North America & international
toll-free: 1 888 232 4444 (USA & Canada)
phone: 250 383 6864 ♦ fax: 812 355 4082

Contents

INTRODUCTION

I started writing poetry when I was about twenty. I was still living at home, had just walked out of art college without completing my course or getting any useful qualifications. I was unemployed, angry at life, longing to escape out into the big wide world but held back by not having a clue as to what I wanted to do or how to do it.. I had few close friends and had learned early in my life to 'keep my own counsel'. Because of this I never showed my writing to anyone.

The first few poems in this collection come from that time. Most need little explanation which is lucky because my memory does not allow me to be certain just why I wrote these words, or who it was I was writing about.. Two poems might however be helped by a little explanation. **'Summer Birth with Joy and Sorrow'** was written shortly after leaving home for the first time and living in a 'Bed Sit' just a mile away from my family home. The piece here is an extract from a much longer poem that, unfortunately is far too embarrassing to publish in its entirety. The second is **'Set My Idle Hands to Work'** which is something between a poem and a prayer. It was written during what seemed like an unending period of unemployment. I was raised Catholic and the legacy of this is still very apparent in the poem although I had stopped going to church as soon as I left my special boarding school at 17 where my church attendance had been compulsory.

Somewhere around the age of 25 I discovered a form of peer counselling founded by a working class man with revolutionary tendencies whom I greatly admired. Probably because I then had the safety and living people to listen to both my thinking and my 'feelings', the need to write poetry to myself seemed to fade, and then stopped for many years.

Despite many new friendships and gaining a direction and a voice in the world, my old habits of keeping many of my inner thoughts private remained with me into my fifties. A particularly close relationship helped me to break out of this, rediscovering the route into my own inner world. Poems again sprang to the surface and had to be written. They were different this time, not so tortured and introspective, and with more to say. Again many are self explanatory, but a few will probably have more meaning if their background is understood.

'The World Stepped Back' is the best description I have for the overwhelming feeling I had as people reacted to the diagnosis of my impairment, Osteogenesis Imperfecta, when I was four days old. Many will say infants of this age cannot remember such things, but I did. Trying to bridge the gap between me and the stepped-back people has been my life's work ever since, not really by choice but by necessity.

'Let Me Cry' was inspired by two events which happened within a day of each other. The first was someone telling me how a small group of friends/counsellors had gathered around a mother and her newly born baby who had cried for the first 24 hours of his life. The people in the group had not only felt their attention had been very useful to the mother and baby, but it had been a privilege for them, albeit very tiring.

The second event was sitting outside (another) café in the early afternoon at what must have been the end of a local 'One O' Clock Club' for mothers and babies. There were maybe 8 or 9 babies accompanied by assorted adults sitting relaxedly in the sun, rocking small bodies or prams, sipping coffee and chatting whilst many of the young ones opened their little mouths and wailed. As I sat there with this chorus drifting up into the blue sky to disperse into the universe it struck me how natural it is to cry, and how little opportunity most of us get to do it. If most mothers could stay so delighted with their noisy offspring as these seemed to be able to do, that day at least, or if friends would gather to help out when it gets hard for them, then what a different sort of world we would have.

'The Café on the Common' is one of my favorite places to think and write. When I first wrote this poem I gave a copy of it to the Italian owner who works there seven days a week despite being officially retired. Recently he confided in me that whenever he reads the poem, he cries. "I don't know why!" he claims, but I think it is to do with having all his hard work appreciated. This to me is a successful poem! The cover photograph was taken there.

Did I Ever Thank You Dad? Was written for my Father who had been a fireman (and painter/decorator/gardener on his days 'off') all through m childhood. He died prematurely at the age of 65 of a heart attack – a common fate of people who work in the fire-service. He never met my daughter or read this poem. I have much to thank him for.

'Forms of Torture' was written after applying for Housing Benefit. Everyone who has applied for Housing Benefit, or any other State Benefit, understands this poem. I know because of the near hysterical laughter from some members of the audience as I read it. It is similar to the experience I try to describe in **'Paper Jam'** and increasingly when I foolishly try to use money from my own bank account, but this is a poem yet to be written.

'Ma Petite Isle de Maurice' is about my mother's homeland of Mauritius, a small island in the India Ocean. Her own story is yet to be told, still buried in the secretive legacy of colonialism and racism. Some of this poem is factual, and some is conjecture. Although I have not yet been to Mauritius I have become increasingly aware of how her story has impacted the lives of her children and grand children. My connection with Mauritius is surprisingly strong within me.

'Now We Are All Middle Class' was written after reading an article by Tony Blair arguing that the Labour Party no longer needs to worry about representing their traditional membership of the working class because the working class no longer exist! This nonsense is still put out by all the main political parties, but I wanted to write about the result in the hearts and minds of the many people who do the sorts of jobs which, despite keeping us all alive, warm, fed, housed, clothed and cared for, who get up in the middle of the night in the freezing weather to clear the roads of dangerous ice and snow so that the rest of us can get to work in the morning, are still extremely badly paid, have low status and imply that the people who do them are too thick to succeed at school. They (we) are becoming more and more invisible it seems.

'They Do It To Us Twice' is one of my angry poems. It is an attempt to describe how the oppressive society damages people, blames them for their struggles and then oppresses them again through the systems they have set up to supposedly help them, such as the 'Care' system, the Mental Health System and much of what passes as 'Special Education'.

'I've Got To Work Work Work' was a chant which came to me after listening to many working class people talk about how hard it is to rest even though all basic needs have been met. It is best performed with an egg shaker. **'Lili Marlene Sings Back'** is also a song to be sung to the original (English) tune of 'Lili Marlene' by Norman Schultze. I have not had the nerve to do this in public, but don't any of you hold back.

'Beware the Baubles' refers to a trend I saw in the well meaning attempts of mainstream teachers and staff to bring the trappings of 'Special Education' into their schools as they opened their doors to children with more significant impairments. Apart from the little known fact that there is a massive 'Special Needs Industry' which make enormous profits from bamboozling people into thinking that those sort of children need really expensive kit such as Sensory Rooms to be included when in fact they often just need a few carpentry skills and a bit of imagination, it misses the main point of inclusive education which is to make 'ordinary' life accessible to those children who need it most but have had it denied through segregated services. I was afraid the disabled children would end up isolated with their 'carers' in the sensory room despite being in the mainstream. Luckily, the prohibitive costs of such specialist equipment and the common sense of teachers and children have modified this trend so that some extra resources are bought, such as ball pools, and used by all the children including those children for whom other equipment would not be accessible.

'Get Better For Mummy' erupted from within after I recalled a party I had attended at a friend's house. A very distressed and very drunk woman seemed attracted to me, an obviously disabled woman, like a magnet. She told me several times during the evening that she had had to put her young disabled child into an institution because he was a 'Dud'. As the tears flowed she said it was the knowledge that he would never speak to her and call her 'Mummy' that had made it impossible for her to keep him at home. At the time I had wanted to put her out of her misery by drowning her in her gin and tonic, but with some later maturity I came to understand why parents can get so confused by the medical model of disability. I wrote this poem to try to put over how a disabled child feels when confronted by such idea. It is still a hard poem for me to read.

'Uppity Downs' is a reflection on what I have learned from my many friends with Down Syndrome. The references in the first verse are to Charles Darwin and his cousin Sir Francis Galton who misdirected Darwin's theory of natural selection to create his eugenics movement. This called for, and led to, the mass institutionalization of thousands of disabled and/or working class people labelled as 'Feeble-minded' in order to prevent them 'Repeating their type' by breeding. John Langdon Down was the medic who noticed certain similar features in a number of inmates, such as eye shape which, he believed, indicated that they were a genetic throwback to an earlier, inferior, asian tribe, thus coining the term 'Mongoloid' to describe them – a term no longer in common usage. Hitler is on the list because he studied eugenics in Britain and the USA as a precursor to his own Final Solution.

'Not Dead Yet' I wrote when asked to speak at a lobby of MPs and Lords who were to be voting on Lord Joffe's latest attempt to legalise 'Assisted Suicide'. Naturally it puts forward the thinking of disabled people, for many of whom the issue is to **stay alive**, not pop our clogs prematurely at the hands of another. I did get to read this poem to a massed crowd outside the Houses of Parliament, but was too nervous to notice the microphone held somewhere near my mouth as I spoke. I was amazed and delighted therefore to be congratulated by many on my poem which had been broadcast on the radio that morning without my knowing.

'Not Dead Yet' is the name of an international campaign of disabled people set up to resist any legalized killing of sick or disabled people:
www.theresistancecampaign.org.uk

'The Rehabilitation Ward' is about a particular ward at the Stanmore Orthopedic Hospital in Middlesex, England. The hospital runs a three week course on pain management for people who need help with chronic pain from surgery, injuries or impairments. The course is very demanding and potential attendees have to undergo two assessments, both physical and psychological, one locally, and a second one by Stanmore itself before they are accepted. They come from all over the UK including Northern Ireland, often having to stay in hotels at the weekends when the ward closes. The commitment is big, but so are the rewards. I go into the ward for three days to have a regular treatment involving an intravenous drip so I only watch. I do not participate except to add my cheers to their efforts when I can.

Inviting the Thieves Back In refers to the extraordinary outcome of the last General Election in Britain in 2010. This led to a coalition government in which no less than eight members of the Cabinet were educated at Eton, one of our most prestigious, and expensive, public schools. Many of them are millionaires including the Prime Minister. The 'statistics' cited come from several publications including the 'Spirit Level' by Richard Wilkinson and Kate Pickett (2009), and 'Injustice – Why Social Equality Still Exists' by Daniel Dorling (2010). They show that from after the first world war, and accelerating after the second world war, social inequalities were leveling out in most developed countries including ours, with improvements in both standard of living and quality of life for working people (whether they were employed, unemployed or retired), women, ethnic minorities, gay and lesbian people, and disabled people up until the 1970s when they reached their peak. Since that time the gap between the rich and poor has been growing again. The research shows that the prevalence of all social problems correlate to, or mirror, this rise in inequality, and imply that they are caused by it.. There is much evidence to show that this has been deliberately engineered by the threatened wealthy to protect themselves.

I use the term 'thieves' to remind us that all wealth is created by the working class of the world, the majority of whom are forced to live on less than $2 a day, or from the appropriation by a few of land and resources which once belonged to us all.

Early Poems (1970 – 1978)

Early Poems (1970 - 1979)

After Tearing Up All the Others

Each time I take up my pen
I mean to write of sunshine
But somehow my hand again
Puts tears in every line –
It is not true! It is a lie!
I am searching for the key
We do not agree, my hand and I
What is you and what is me.
Meanwhile my friends look up
Gaze deep into the sky
There is no time for sadness
There is no need to cry –
One day I will find the words to tell
My hand to write what is real
That day I'll scream and sing and yell
And express the way I feel.

1970

Summer Birth with Joy and Sorrow

In the stillness of my new home
In the peace of silent quarters
My bottled thoughts come seeping outwards
Like a timid baby rabbit
Slowly, quietly, looking, listening
Anxiously ready to fly back inward
Into the safety of the subconscious
But now no longer crushed and bleeding
By the walls of misunderstanding
But free and naked my soul is reborn
Protected and nurtured by friends so gentle
Who understand the need to live.

1973

Come Out From the Shadows

To live alone is not possible for me
From my walls come echoes of my other self
Louder than any other sound
Which is but an answer to the eternal spirit
Who calls on me when all else is quiet
Whose presence is often more real
Than a crowd of human beings
Who may not be real at all with me
Yes, sometimes this voice is frightening
But always exciting, vital, free
Full of wisdom and light
Oftentimes people hide from this being
Running to the deadness of life
To company, noise, ceaseless activity
To sleep and talk and mindless prose
Running like an insect away from the light
To hide beneath a heavy stone –
The light shines to make things clear
To show you the lines, the form, the beauty
Shade your eyes and come out from the shadows

1973

Set My Idle Hands to Work

Please set my idle hands to work
That my heart may beat in rhythm
With life's heart
That I need no longer stand still
Twisting and turning in my confusion
Whilst the busy people walk by me
Peaceful and serene in their mighty tasks –
I know there is much to be done
And too few willing to leave behind their chains and
fetters
To plow the fields of heaven
With the beautiful sweat of honest brows –
But I wish with all my heart
To plunge my hands into the soil
To move it piece by piece
By the strength of my love
Until all is ready for the new season
Of life and growth and ripening –

I do not understand
Why I am so afraid
To undo my handcuffs

To open the doors of my self imposed prison
To leave behind those who have no need of me
To walk out into the unknown
Alone
As we all must
To seek myself in the shadows and the stars
To find my place in the movement of life
When I do not believe it is possible to miss –

It is just my fear that I will not be used
In the great plan that You have drawn
Because I am not worthy to hold
Your precious tools
But I will not know
Until I open my hands
Of Your great generosity.

1975

(Untitled)

I knew as a young child
Nine to be exact
That it didn't really matter
That the outside wasn't straight
Or big, or strong, or beautiful
And pained the eyes of others
Because bones cannot cry
And skin cannot love
And muscles do not move
Unless moved
By the force from the inside
That grows unfettered
By physical bounds
Fed by the same emotions as others

Living in the same world
With the same multitude
Of joys and sorrows
Ranged before me
To choose as I will
And the same capacity for happiness
As anyone
Who has dug deep their cup
With tools fashioned themselves
From life's invisible steel
With wide open eyes
And a wide open heart

1975

Naked

Have you ever thought
How much more naked than naked
It is possible for people to be?
While almost anyone it is true
Could strip you of your clothes
How many could undress your heart
Your mind and soul lay bare?
And have you ever thought
If you could do the same?
If someone could trust you that much
He would allow the walls to tumble
All the defenses sent home
Leaving his raw self visible
There for you to touch?
Do you get embarrassed
To see such nudity?

Or do you gasp in wonder
That such a gift is held up to you
And to be worthy
And gentle enough to hold
Someone else's being
To understand what it is you see
And reward this open person
With the self same honesty?
Have you ever thought how many people never
know
Anything else but skin-deep visions
Of people, and life, and love?

1974

Late Summer

The startling, sparkling streaming sun
Floods the landscape goldly.
The flickering, fluttering, feathery wind
Stirs the paints quite boldly
Whilst humming, buzzing, rustling things
Gyrate in dance,
Endure a glance
Create a trance
And take care of us so oldly

Shimmering silver sunlight
Switches on summer madness
Filling blue airy skies
With intangible summer gladness
While colours shine
Like mellow wine
All yours and mine
To melt away our sadness

1971

My Spring Poem

Blossom's comin' out
Flowers comin' out
Sun's comin' out –
I made it again!
Spring is in the air
Wind is in m' hair
Easter's got its Fair
Now there aint no despair
'Cos I made it again!
Buds are on the trees
They'll soon be baby leaves
Fluttrin' in the breeze
I should be on my knees
'Cos I made it again!
Winter's packed his things
An' all the cold he brings
Jack Frost no longer sings
Yes, I've made it again!

Sparrers are bouncing around on the ground
Their legs aint so strong but their voices are sound
And there's things that I've lost and things that I've found
Though no one can tell me just to where 'tis I'm bound
I'm glad
Sometimes sad
Maybe mad
But I made it again!

1974

Later Poems (2003 – 2011)

The World Stepped Back

Once I was an ordinary baby
Chubby arms
Tiny fingernails
A shock of hair
Someone to be loved
Cuddled and sung to
Bathed and fed
Close to my mother
A bright future ahead
I felt safe

I was an ordinary baby
For four short days
Before the cold table
The huge camera
The radiographer's skill
Revealed my hidden secret

And the world stepped back
Abandoning me
To forces we could not fight
Larger than love
Judgment
A redefining of my value
A bleak future
All delight snuffed out
Like a light

What could I make of this
Left to scream
In my hospital cot
I felt irredeemably flawed
Flailing in space
My future in doubt

My Daddy's eyes saved me
Green and sparkly
The delight came back
As we looked and looked
The connection once made
Could not be broken
The look reminded me
I had once felt safe
And I knew,
Somehow I knew
He would come back one day
Not just to visit
But to take me home

2007

Let Me Cry

I have just come into the world
And I need to cry
I need to cry long and loud
I need to recover from my journey here
Struggles you will never know
I need to howl and scream
Not for what is ahead
Or for what is now
But for all that was behind

I entered a world full of history
Broken hearts, forgotten dreams,
Fights, pain, loss and damage
Fears and disappointments
I can see them in your eyes
Behind the love

The legacy of misguided actions,
Oppression, suppression and war
Unhealed and passed on intact
From one generation to the next
And so on down the line
I see it in your eyes
And if I am not to have to look away
Let me cry for us all

Don't try to stop me
Like you were stopped
With dummies and distractions,
Shouts and threats,
Shakes and violence
Until the fear of your reaction
Teaches me to crush myself
Into a silent ball of pain

This pain will poison my mind
Chill my heart
Block out the present
Make me ill
Stop me thinking
Make me afraid
Of my own feelings
Leaving me small and impaled
Condemned to eternally search for a Someone
Who knows
I need to cry

If you let me cry,
Stay with me and welcome my tears
I can dissolve a thousand years of grief
Keep ownership of my mind
Notice the love still in your eyes
The gentleness of your touch
Your efforts to remain close
Your hope reborn with me

I will feel the joy of living
In a breathtaking world of beauty
Amongst peoples of awesome courage
Yearn to live each moment well
Holding nothing back

And when I become an adult
And you yourself are in need
I will be able to hold you
Whilst you cry
Remind you of your goodness
Thank you for all you have done
Forgive your imperfections
Caress your aged body
Look deep into your eyes
Be still and quiet
Beside you and with you
For as long as you need me to
I will let you cry

2007

In Praise of Subjectivity

I know what I know
Because I have lived it
Smelled it, heard it,
Felt it, seen it.

I know what I know because I held hands
Witnessed the stories,
Felt the pain, wiped up the blood,
Cried the tears,
With others,
Many others.

I know what I know because I have reflected
On all these stories
Talked about them,
Laughed about them,
Thought about them,
Drawn conclusions,
Tried things out,
Made mistakes,
Tried again.

You know what you know
Because you have read it,
Attended the lectures,
Written the essays,
Passed the exams,
Gained professional status
Distance and
Objectivity.

Your word is sought out,
Trusted and valued,
Handsomely paid.

Mine is ignored,
Silenced,
Starved of resources
Dismissed in my
Subjectivity,
My passion, tears and rage.

Thus

Those who know (but think they don't)

Are condemned to be controlled

By those

Who could never know (but think they do).

2005

The Other End of the Banana

I was struggling with the stalk end
To unpeel the stubborn banana
But the skin was too thick,
The stalk too bendy
I had no knife to help my quest
When my friend, seeing my plight
Leaned over and turned the banana around.
Nipping off the little black cap she said
"See, a banana is weaker at the other end –
I wasn't born in Africa for nothing".
As I then easily peeled back the thinner skin
I wondered why
In fifty five years
It had never occurred to me
That I could try the other end.

The Café on the Common

There is a café I like
On Tooting Bec Common.
It is an outside café.
A Café which welcomes those of us
Who are often not made welcome inside Cafés

Elderly people out for a breathe of air
On scooters
Disabled people with big wheelchairs
Parents with young children
In all manner of buggies,
Tricycles, bicycles and carts,
And people who own dogs
Of every shape, size and colour
All come to sit at the Café
Under the oaks
Looking across the broad green
Sipping drinks
And soaking up the sun

The food is simple, homely and good.
They ask me how my daughter is
When they bring it out to me.
They remember that I do not take sugar
In my tea.

I recall one special day
When the rain came suddenly down
We all crushed into the small veranda
Ten dripping people,
Fifteen steaming dogs
The close proximity sparking conversation
"What do you do?"
"I work for inclusion"
"Oh Yes, That would be good"
I listened to a story of a life
Forever shaped by remembered cruelty
Towards a left-handed child
Living in a right-handed world.
A surprise gift
On a wet day.

The Cafe is full of life,
Dogs barking, running for sticks,
Children laughing,
Adults talking,
Teenagers rollerblading past.
There seems to be room for us all
Outside.

2004

In Her Own Time

She was wearing Wellington boots
With bright stripes of red, black, orange and white
Made for jumping in puddles
And she had found one
A big one
Deep and dark and muddy
Just waiting for her

But her family were in a hurry, already walking away
"Anna, come on, it is time to go!"

Anna did not follow
She was completely enchanted by her study.
Stepping slowly into the deepest spot
She watched the water ripple away from her feet.
She stepped forwards.
More ripples appeared and disappeared.
She turned and kicked at the water.
Thousands of droplets
Showered the path
Leaving black dots shining in the sun.

But her family were impatient to be moving on.
"I've told you already. We will leave you here if you
don't come now!"

Anna closed her ears.
She was enthralled by her study.
She turned and kicked the other way
Harder
But into the grass so as not to splash the passers by.
Stepped into a second puddle
In the grass
Muddier
Squelching deliciously beneath her stamp
Now one foot, now the other
Sinking and sucking at her boots
She held up her skirt
And ran laughing through the puddle

"Anna!" The voice got louder, angrier,
"Come on this minute!"

Anna looked down at the water.
She was transfixed by its' secrets.
She turned away from the insistent calling.
A figure came chasing
She ran away, round the edge of the puddle
Just flustering the water all around
He snatched her out of her enquiry
Swung her under his arm
Her wet boots flailing at the sky
Wailing and beating her fists
She is marched away from her puddle
And her joy in learning
In her own time

2004

Did I Ever Thank You Dad?

Did I ever thank you Dad
For looking at me with such delight
Whilst all others were wringing their hands
Lost in the deadly imagined tragedy
Of the Brittle Bone Baby
Your sparkling green eyes alone
Sent me a life-line
A connection so brief
But strong enough to anchor me
Through those terrifying whispered half-lit hospital
nights
Knowing
You would come to my rescue

Did I ever thank you Dad
For all the skills you learnt
Through grueling apprenticeships
Employed for our comfort, security and peace
Sleeves rolled up, sawing and hammering,
Plastering and painting
Digging and planting,
Stripping down and mending

Labouring at work
Labouring at home
Seldom resting
Whistling, tired and proud

Did I ever thank you Dad
For the games, the cuddles, the jokes
For carrying me on your shoulders
Riding me on your bike
Our harmonica playing funny man
My sister and I
Rolled up with laughter
In nonsense bed time fun

Did I ever thank you Dad
For telling me that you were content
That we seemed to be enough for you
Worth all the energy you spent
You treasured us all
Though the world saw me with pity
You saw me with pride
Your artist, your thinker, your fighter

I saw never saw shame in your eyes

Your big heart gave out too soon Dad
So much success you didn't see
Grandchildren you never met
You were worn out by childhood hunger
Being a soldier in an unwanted war
Three jobs to make ends meet
A fireman hero rushing into danger
When all others are rushing out
Always being brave
Always being
A man.

2006

Forms of Torture

I am referring here not to forms
In the category sense
But in the paper sense,
In the duplicate, triplicate, fill-me-in-or-else sense
Use-capital-letters-and-black-ink-sense,
In the attach-your-proof-here sense
In the do-it-right-or-we-will-close-your-case sense
That only poor, sick or desperate people know.

To begin with they do not tell us that we can get
some help.
We have to find that out ourselves.
That is OUR responsibility we are told.

Then you have to have the RIGHT form with a
corresponding number
Available on request from the CORRECT office
Open Mon-Thurs but only after lunch and not on
bank holidays
Or STAFF TRAINING DAYS

Or you can phone and ask for one to be sent
Leave your name and address
And WAIT
Then ring again when you can be sure
The person you spoke to will not be there
And, unlike the responsible person you will now be speaking to,
Didn't make a note or do anything.

The forms will eventually arrive,
But the deadline and your debts will be looming.
Social workers are no longer trained to help claimants.
Benefits advisers will help
If you go in person
To make an appointment
But they are VERY busy.

You decide to go it alone

Take a deep breath,

Open it up, black pen at the ready.

Name, address

(I can do that)

What Are Your Needs?

(It depends which day we are talking about)

How Much Did You Earn In the Last Financial Year?

(Not enough, obviously)

What Have You Saved, and Where?

(Does my piggy bank count?)

About Your Partner

(Do you mean that creep snoring in the back
bedroom?)

Can You Attach PROOF of Everything?

Photocopies of all those papers you should have filed
away

But didn't
(Where the hell is my Birth Certificate anyway?)
Do you have a Doctors Certificate
(She's on annual leave until the Spring)

You are beginning to lose the will to live
But it is not over yet.
With an exhausted but triumphant flick,
The envelope falls into the letter box,
And you anxiously await the confirmation
Necessary for you to pay your rent,
For your food,
Your children's clothes,
To stay warm
But it doesn't come.

You go down in desperation but they have no record
Of receiving a claim from you.
Have you PROOF OF POSTING?
Did you keep a COMPLETE PHOTOCOPY?
No!?
Well it must have got lost in the system
We will send you another
But of course without PROOF of posting
There can be NO BACKDATING.
It will be treated as a fresh claim.
It is not our fault.
That is the way the system works.
We have to guard against FRAUD.
You know what YOU PEOPLE ARE LIKE.
If you want to complain,
Pick up a form on your way out.

Let's Pretend

You are richer than me
I am richer than him
You can wear jumpers from Harrods
I buy my clothes in Next

I can eat avocados
In the warm
He goes hungry
In the cold

Let's pretend we don't see it
Let's pretend we are the same

If we speak about our clothes
I might start to hate you
If we speak about my food
He might start to hate me

I might want your clothes
He might want my food

I might think you do not deserve your clothes
He might think I do not deserve my food

We would have a million reasons
To defend our selves from sharing what we have
All of them lies
Born out of fear

It is so much easier
To talk about the weather

2005

Me, Sparrows and the Meaning of Life

When I was just a little child
I was put outside for air
Each day parked by the geraniums
Left to sit and stare

From the sky my friends would come
Sparrows small and sweet
They fluttered and chirruped and bounced
Playing games around my feet

Animated little works of art
I delighted as they played
They showed no fear of me I learned
If no sudden move I made

I liked it when the rain came down
Rustling wind the birds would chase
Blowing their feathers, blowing my hair
Wetting my hands and face

My mother usually saw the storm
Hauling me quickly inside
"Why didn't you call?" she would plaintively wail
With reproachful silence I replied

Now sparrows are in decline they say,
No explanation has been found
How can I help my childhood friends
To once again abound?

I feel somehow our difficulties
Are part of the same demise
Sparrows, tigers, you and me
Together we fall, or together we rise

Ma Petite Isle de Maurice

I have said the words so often
In response to queries about my name
"My Mother comes from Mauritius"
And there the explanation stops
Crash lands
A hidden story not to be told
The twisted tangled shameful story
Of sugar.

The once wild, uninhabited Island
Silver sands, lush tropical leaves,
Giant Water lilies and pink pigeons
The Dodo now famous
Only because it is dead
Eaten to extinction by the white settlers
Greedy for food and land
Whose vivid imaginations could easily envisage
Field upon field of waving sugar cane
Replacing the tropical forests
They claimed as their own.

They sent out their boats to Africa,
India and beyond
The Dutch, the French, the British,
To capture their labour force
Slaves for Tate and Lyle
And, not content to exploit the men
Raped the women and so created
The perfect middle class
Mixed race children they believed they could educate
To manage the plantations
Separated from their mothers
Given a new identity
Records not kept
History unwritten
Given European names
To disguise their heritage
A pale skinned sub-culture
Poor as dirt
But no longer slaves
Keeping the secret
Denying their past

Clinging to each other
And the bitter fragments of privilege
The evil pact of colonial rule
From this deceitful history
I was born
My mother's daughter
Now living in England
Unable to speak of her own father
Of his fifteen children
His brutality and superstitions
Arising from his untold story
Our roots firmly buried
Beneath the stamped down soil
Of the fields of sugar

My mother created her own island
Tried to make us live in it
For safety
All memories spoken in French or Creole
Between her brothers and sisters
Shutting out her husband and children
By language and custom

She tried to bury the past
Instilling in us a fear of history
Don't ask, don't think
Don't speak ill of the dead
Leaving the pain frozen in memories
Passed down through the generations
Unhealed
And less understandable

As it re-emerges
Seemingly disconnected from its source
To corrupt our closest relationships
Guarded, secretive, deeply confused
Our identities defined only in the negative
We are not white
We are not black
Condemned to be eternal outsiders
Weeping for a story we will never know
Yet at last I can feel the connection
With the silver sands, the pink pigeons
The giant tortoises upon whose back

My mother told me,
You can take the slowest ride
With the wonderful mixture of peoples –
African, Indian, Chinese and European
Because they all live on within me
Inextricably interwoven
Then, now and forever
With ma petite Isle de Maurice.

2007

More is Less

I cannot help but wonder
Why the poor and struggling peoples
Scratching their existence
From thin and barren means
Look so alive
Whilst those of us
Who labour to maintain our mountains
Of wealth and privilege
Look so dead

2007

Now We Are All Middle Class

Ten A-C's
Preferably with stars
That is the only way to be
Successful now,
It's the only point of school

The stiff competition
In the global market
Makes it necessary you see
To raise the standards
To such a degree
That we can all be free
Of the need
To be working class

No, we won't need houses
Hospitals or schools.
Buildings are now unnecessary
And so are tools.
No bricks will need laying
No pipes to be plumbed,

No wood to join,
No tiles to be laid,
No walls to be plastered,
No sockets to be wired.
No roads, no rails,
No phone lines, cables or masts.
All that is in the past now
We are no longer working class

No more oil rigs,
No more gas,
No more wind power
Turbines, generators or grids
No more electricity,
Petrol at the pumps,
No more servicing or maintenance
No more mechanics for our cars,
No more clothes to be sewn
No more washing, ironing or putting away,
No more hair to be cut.
Nothing will need making,
And nothing will ever break,

All that is in the past now
We are no longer working class

No more babies to be cuddled,
No more patients to be healed,
No more Home Care, Child Care or Meals on wheels,
No more sadness to be noticed,
No more messes to be cleaned,
No more food to be farmed,
No more meals to be cooked
No more heat, no more light,
No more deaths to be grieved
The future is in the City
Now that we are all middle class

2003

They Do It To Us Twice

They do it to us twice, their trick.
First they send out their battalions
To find us when we are innocent and new,
And still full of hope
Then set upon us until we are battered and bruised
Bleeding all over our own dreams
Firing away at our beauty
Our power and our strength
By judgments
Criticism and lies
Exclusion from the fold
Systems that rob and exploit
Which render us powerless
Until we are weak and full of holes
Misshapen and small
Barely able to think
We bow to the rulers
The Powers That Be.
We know they are there
Though we seldom see them

Then, when we lift our scarred and injured bodies
Off the battle floor
Turning mistakenly for help
To the same people, now in a fresh disguise,
They condemn us for our wounded appearance
Our pain now the excuse to unleash upon us
A second battalion
To seal in the victory of the first.

They send out their agents
Trained to seem nice
Authority cloaked in kindness
Coming to assess their damage
Hating us now because we are broken
Because we have absorbed their violence
And turned it upon ourselves.
They blame and fear their cornered victims
Filling in their forms
Case conferences
To decide our fate

Run from them, the experts!
All those who think they know what is wrong with us
And how we need to be modified
So that we can be jammed
Into those little boxes
They carved out for us
Before we were born.

Beware the therapists
The programmes and the pills.
Their Special Schools,
Secure Units,
Locked wards,
Prison cells
Are all built in denial
Of the havoc they created
In our minds and bodies
Still earning their living off our pain

Look only to each other
Listen with all your heart!
Listen to your brother
Your sister, all those near
Your comrades, your friends
Your children
Those who have suffered with us
Who know inside
There is nothing wrong with us.
There was never anything wrong with us.
It is simply justice we need
To put an end to their trick.

2003

I've Got To Work Work Work

I've got to work work work
Or be a jerk jerk jerk
I must not shirk shirk shirk
I've got to work work work

I've got to strive strive strive
To stay alive live live
I must not hive hive hive
I've got to strive strive strive

I must not rest rest rest
Life is a test test test
Must do my best best best
I must not rest rest rest

I mustn't stop stop stop
Until I drop drop drop
Pass me that mop mop mop
I musn't stop stop stop

I've got to try try try
Until I die die die
Not asking why why why
I've got to try try try

I've got to work work work
Or be a jerk jerk jerk
I must not shirk shirk shirk
I've got to work work work work work work work
work ...

2007

Self Doubt

Listen, I've got a great idea!
Does it make sense?
Am I right?
Did I miss the point?
Is it a bit naff?
Have I understood?
Was that silly?
Did you laugh at me?
Am I wrong?
Should I have even tried?
Is there someone who knows?
I expect there is.
I am sorry
I wasted your time.

2003

Sorry, I Don't Have the Time

I am sorry about your broken heart
It is a pity it was this week
my diary is full of urgent things
I should be doing as we speak

My MOT, I know it is late
My computer is on the blink,
Bills to pay, Tax returns,
Plates screaming from the sink

A report to write, my boss is firm
The deadline must be met
A stack of post, my inbox full
New targets to be set

In three weeks time, at half past five
I can see a little space
I'll squeeze you in, I'll hold you close
Though at seven I must race

I didn't choose to live like this
The pace is set elsewhere
I cannot afford to be left behind
I cannot afford to care

When Language Becomes a Tool of Oppression

I came to share with you my thinking
Eager to communicate new ideas
But how fragile they were
Beneath the torrent of words
I seemed to provoke
l-o-n-g and obscure
And so many of them!
My own words transformed to armour
Trying to protect my mind
From the merciless bombardment of sound
Failing, my voice was silenced
Like so many times before
Until my aching brain was jammed
All thought grinding to a halt

Stupified
I just wanted to hit you
Gave up, walked away
Did you feel triumph?
Or did you wonder what went wrong
As you employed all the verbal skills
You have been trained in all your life
To defend your class position
Your objective reasoning
Your professional distance
Your intellectual superiority
In your futile attempt to help?

Things I Don't Need

I don't need fashion magazines
30 pairs of shoes or a Prada- Handbag
Eyelash curlers
Stick-on nails
Cosmetics or designer perfumes
Gold chains or fancy jewelery
Streaks in my hair or false nails
Botox, Liposuction or a facelift

I don't need cheeseburgers
With extra cheese and bacon
Fish and chips
Crème Brulee, chocolate fudge cake
Or roast suckling pig with cranberry jus

I don't need Coca Cola, Dr Pepper
Tango, Sprite or 7Up
Or any other chemically flavoured, sugar-laden fizzy
drinks

I don't need alcohol, cigarettes, speed or weed ,
Prozac. Ritalin or Seroxat
To numb me to my pain
And halt my recovery

I don't need to hoard great collections of stuff
In my loft, basement or garage -
In fact I don't need a loft, basement or garage,
A mortgage
Or to buy more than I can afford

I don't need Blue Ray, a Blackberry or a web cam,
An I Pod or a WII
Or to download my 50,000 favourite tunes onto
anything

I don't need life insurance, a personal pension plan,
Extended warranties or lifetime guarantees
To bring me peace of mind

I don't need qualifications, degrees,
Gongs, titles or fame
To entitle me to respect
But

I do need
Enough food, warmth and shelter to be healthy
I do need
To know I am loved even if my mind should grow
cloudy and my body fail,
I do need
Attention to think and to be creative,
I do need
To be able to delight in the natural world around me,
I do need
To feel a hand in mine when I am lost or afraid,
I do need
A community and a purpose
Such human things
So hard to find

2004

Your Computer Doesn't Love You

Your computer doesn't love you
Nor does your mobile phone
Your I Pod doesn't give a damn
Your TV has no sensuous zone

Yet you gaze at them for hours
Listen to their every sound
Paying them rapt attention
The perfect partner it seems you've found

The workplace has gone silent
Save for the ring tones, buzzes and clicks
The stories, the laughter, the ideas
Replaced by a clock as it ticks

Home is of a similar nature
Everyone in a room of their own
Intimate with an electronic companion
Whilst actually completely alone

Look at me! Hear my voice!
You can talk to me for free
I can respond to you, think with you
I am real! I am real! I am real!

Cyberspace is not the real world
Electrons are not human beings
Don't be fooled by a full In-Box
It is isolation, not connection we are seeing

The Myth of Choice

They own all the resources,
They write all the rules,
They create all the systems,
But they know we're not fools

To be so controlled
We would never agree
So they have to persuade us
We are noble and free

Within their prisons
They let us choose many things
Bread or potatoes
Roundabouts or swings

They trumpet our causes
They are so on our side
Our right to more segregation
Or assisted suicide

We don't feel too grateful
We still seem quite vexed,
But their slippery words
Just keep us perplexed

It suits them to pit us
Against our best mates,
So we don't join together
To decide our own fates

I know this sounds simple,
A naïve little rhyme,
But equality, not choice,
Will make freedom be mine

2005

The Harmonica Man

I heard it before
As I drove past, stuck at the lights,
A beautiful, haunting tune
Played on a harmonica
Floating through my window.
I turned and glimpsed the old man
Sitting on the ground
Sharing perhaps the only skill
He has left
Before the traffic moved me on.

I was glad to see him again
Sitting outside Sainsbury's
Silent, staring sadly into some invisible thought
His harmonica laid flat on the pavement.

Will you play for me I asked.
His face came to life.
What would you like he asked.
You choose something I said.
I looked at his face, so tired, so sad,
Neatly clipped beard

His thin hands shaking.
As he started to play
His feet began to tap out a rhythm
From some remembered time
When life had been different.
For him.

I wanted to put my arm round him.
Stroke his hands.
His dignity touched me.
Who loves this man
Playing beautiful music
Into the air?
Who is he? What has he seen?
Why am I so frozen and scared
That I can only thank him for his gift,
Give him a few coins,
And not touch
And not ask?

2004

Paper Jam

I've got a paper jam in my brain
Caused by too many insurance certificates,
Extended warranties and tax returns
Parking tickets, timesheets and monitoring forms
Bank Statements, Invoices and receipts
Spreadsheets and reconciliations
Renewals and applications
A never ending sea of demands
Arriving relentlessly through the post

The paper in my in-tray breeds
It multiplies at night
Clogging up my creativity
Colonising my life with staples,
Photocopies, ring binders and box files
Cluttering up my tables and shelves
Spilling from one surface to another
Attracting marmalade and coffee cup rings
Whilst the only thing I really need
Sticks itself to the bottom of something else
Which I unknowingly throw in the bin
Requiring hours of future searching

The threat of fines or prison
Whipping me into submission
A paper slave.

I have better uses for all this paper

We could for instance
Fold a thousand paper hats
Stick them on our heads at jaunty angles
Go watch football in the rain

We could let loose a flotilla of paper boats
In streams under bridges
Rushing from side to side
To see whose little prow comes out first

We could cut out a pile of paper snowflakes
Make a giant snowstorm
Tear a million pieces of confetti
Throw them from a high building on a windy day
In case someone is getting married

Let us paste a thousand pieces onto a huge balloon
Pop it
Leaving a perfect papier-mâché ball
Ready to be painted bright colours,
Roll it down a hill
With us following

Let us draw our dreams in felt-tip pens
Stick them all over the Town Hall
Ask for comments

Let us write each other appreciations
Read them aloud to people who need them
Hide them in their clothes and lunch boxes

Let us paper some houses on the outside
Attach bags full of pens
Invite our neighbours, their children
And all overlooked people
To put up their thoughts for all to see

Let us gather all the reams of paper waiting
To be covered in the Daily Newspoison
Scrunch it all up
Stuff it instead into our eco-friendly cavity walls
To keep us warm in winter

Let us take all the test and exam papers filling our
schools
Add them to our carrot scrapings and potato skins
Make sumptuous compost for our gardens and
allotments
Grow something nourishing for our ailing bodies

Let us release our clerical brothers and sisters
From the straight jackets of bureaucracy
Retrain them in the ancient art of paper folding
Create an enormous flock of peace cranes
Glue them to the walls of the Ministry of Defense
Sing together our songs of hope

Let us take those fashion magazines
Condemning our baggy clothes and matching
bodies
Cut them into glossy coloured leaf shapes
Stick them to some painted branches
Turn them back to trees

Can't you just feel your mind opening up
Divested of the last screwed-up, ink-sodden wads
Leaving it free to work as nature intended
Our memories, our imaginations,
Our freedom of thought coming back to life
Oh bliss.

2007

Lili Marlene Sings Back

Underneath the lantern by the Barrack gates
There I met a soldier afraid of what awaits
I was his refuge from the fear
He held me near, shed a tear,
Some comfort in the lamplight
From his own Lili Marlene

I tried to be of service, to bring a gentle touch
My body pressed against him,
It didn't seem like much
But when he kissed me my love did start
Though soon to part, he won my heart
Sheltered in the lamplight
By his own Lili Marlene

Now the roll call is over, it is time for him to go
The battle fields are waiting, his blood is soon to flow
Please tell me why good men must die
Their women sigh, break down and cry
Deserted in the lamplight
Endless Lili Marlenes

Beware the Baubles

They stole away our lives
Condemned us to a bean-bag existence
Alone together with our fellow prisoners
Left staring at mobiles, slowly moving round and
round,
Just out of reach

Over-controlled teaching
In a hush of false protection
They pared down our experiences
To their diet of force-fed crumbs
Of learning

Not broken–down, but shattered
Stripped of all meaning and context
By their one-step-at-a-time Special Curriculum
Practicing for the life
They would never let begin

Now they are trying to sell our lives back
Through their glittering, flashing, bubbling rooms
Mechanical, artificial, expensive,
Another capitalist con
Feeding off our starvation

Beware the baubles, the disco dream
The light of the sun will do, thanks,
The brush of the wind, the wet of the rain,
The sound of children's laughter
In an ordinary, busy classroom
The touch of a friends hand
Welcoming us back
Into the world

Life is a multi-sensory experience
Full of lights, tastes, smells
Colours, sounds, textures abounding
Emotions, all our birthright
Denied to us by misunderstanding
And fear

Put away your cheque books
Bring us in close to the beating pulse
Of shared messy, risky, noisy days
Where we all have complex needs
We will learn then all that matters
And so will you.

Get Better for Mummy

Won't you smile for Mummy
Won't you smile and look at me
Won't you look at me and say a word
Just say a word or two
Won't you speak to me and smile
Won't you sit up please
Won't you sit up and smile and speak to me
Won't you ever walk
Won't you stand up and smile and speak to me
Won't you read and write
Won't you do your sums and pass your tests
Won't you stand up and smile and talk and walk and
read and write and pass your tests
For Mummy and Daddy who love you
And don't want you to be tossed away
With the other garbage
Won't you just get better for Mummy and Daddy
So we know we haven't failed you?

                    Won't you smile at me Mummy
          Won't you touch my face and know I can feel you
                    Won't you listen to me Mummy

Speaking without words
Won't you notice that I am happy
Happy when you smile and touch me
Won't you help me to sit up
With soft plump pillows
Won't you lend me your arms and legs
To help me explore the world
Seeking the joy of friendship
Won't you tell the teachers
That words on paper are not the only way
To share our gifts
Won't you tell me you love me Mummy
In all my imperfection
Won't you tell the world Mummy
That human beings do not belong on garbage heaps
But in close communities of learning
Where we all struggle together
Won't you be proud of me Mummy and Daddy
Just the way I am
So I know I haven't failed you?

2005

The Spa School Blues

(Written after watching 'Make Me Normal' featuring four young people with autism who all attend a large State run Special School. Channel 4, June 2nd 2005)

Four beautiful young people
Alive, feeling, wondering why
The world does not seem to want them.

Every day they are sent to Special School
To hear from Jude
And her conspirators
That the world does not want them
Because they are flawed
To the core of their beings
By AUTISM
And their AUTISM won't go away
But will ruin their lives
Unless they practice and practice and practice
Acting like normal people
Special School has a mission it seems
A curriculum based on self hatred.

"I have to drum it into them"
Jude's earnest voice informs us
"What a big and awful thing
Their AUTISM really is".
She needs them to know this, she says,
So they can not expect too much of life.

It works. They are learning.
One looks at the camera and says she has one friend,
Just one friend in the whole world.
"Is life worth living with just one friend?"
She asks.

Another is desperate to have a girl friend
But no young mates to show him the ropes
A third spills her pain all over the playground
Not knowing she is being filmed.
The youngest, just lost his mother to cancer
Climbs into a trunk
And from the dark safety inside
Wonders if his bad behaviour killed her.

Now it is too late, he says,
To tell her he was sorry.

No one comforts, no one reassures,
No one explains that they are good,
Magnificent and courageous,
Interesting and delightful.
No one tells them that they are loved and wanted,
That autism is part of them, like their hair and their
eyes,
Or that it is the world which needs to practice
Carving out the unique places
Each one of us needs
In order to be included,
To live a life amongst people
Who can embrace our differences
And in so doing,
Embrace their own.

Don't make us normal.
Make us welcome.

2005

The Waiting Game

As a very tiny child
I waited a timeless eternity
To be rescued
From motherless danger-filled hospital wards.

At home I was told to wait
To be got up
Taken to the toilet
Fed, washed and dressed
Set down on the floor to play.

Long days stretched before me
Waiting for my sister to come home from school,
Waiting for my Dad to come home from work,
Waiting for my friend to come and play,
Waiting for my Mum to stop being busy
Alone with my dolls
I spent my life waiting.

I was good at waiting
I didn't complain very much
Gradually, not at all
I thought it was what I deserved.

I found a thousand strategies to fill the lonely hours
For which I was greatly praised.

Patience however did not push me up
The pecking order of life
Indeed, alongside so many others
It served to hold me down.

Later, some natural talents
And some helping hands
Helped me to struggle off the ground
Heaving away the leaded lid
Designed to pin me in my designated place
Within the hinterlands of human value.
But I never rose high enough to escape
The endless commands to wait

Not for luxuries you understand,
But for basic needs to be met
"We will give your daughter a bath she can use
If you wait three years"
"You can have a car you can drive"-
Another three years
Just wait
Be patient
Their commands rendered me powerless again and
again.

Then one day it happened
Sitting in my car at the petrol station
Needing someone to give me a hand
To fill her up
I waited, hooted, shouted
Waved my 'help' sign out the window
And everyone walked by or took no notice
Until my reservoir of patience suddenly dried up
And I started up the engine

Threw her into gear
Revved up a mighty power
And drove at 100 miles an hour
Into their plate glass shop front window
Shattering and exploding
Flying bricks
Screams
All mangled up with over priced flowers
Firelighters and barbeque briquettes
Innocent shoppers lying injured and bleeding as I shouted
"I NEED IT NOW!"

The police did not understand
They locked me inside a cell
Told me to wait for the doctor.

2008

Uppity Downs

(Dedicated to Sophie, Kirsty, Joe, Tom, Chloe, Kitty, Anya, Ellen, Charlotte, Nick, Sonny, Luc and Ruby who have all touched my life in different ways and helped me to understand what it means to be fully human.)

I am glad to be able to report
To Messrs Darwin, Galton, Churchill and Down
Hitler and the Third Reich
That your mission was a failure.

Though you tried so hard to persuade us
With your learned accomplices
To believe in your nightmare
Requiring the extermination of the Flawed,
The Flawed have nonetheless flowered.

Protected from your twisted plan
By unstoppable love,
Now released from the ghettos
People with Down Syndrome
And other endangered treasures

Are rising up all over the world
Getting uppity and visible

Artists and poets,
Actors and dancers,
Some quiet and thoughtful,
Some noisy and fun,
A teacher, every one

You could say in fact
That your horrible experiment
Has not simply failed
But gloriously backfired!

Parents all fired up
With fierce and defensive love
For their targeted children
Have joined arms with the Flawed
And other progressive forces
To insist on inclusion for all
Replacing your elitist ideals
Of Empire and Might -

Britain forever Ruling the Waves -
With a different dream
Taking hold in many places
Of a slower, more gentle world
In which being born human is enough
To evoke awe, wonder and respect
From each to all

The end of competition,
The start of collaboration
A bottom-up revolution
Heralding a new world
In which it is safe for all of us
To be our selves.

2007

Not Dead Yet

I have lived to see another spring
To breathe in the blossom's perfumed air
To feel again the sun warming my skin
To wonder at the life we share

I have another chance to notice
Shining eyes meeting my own
Some with love, some with questions
The hope, fear, pain we have all shown

I can touch again those I care for
With my hands, my mind, my heart
They touch me as if for the first time
New thoughts, our dreams just start

Physical pain I have known plenty
Impairment holds little fear for me
But to feel unwanted, a burden, a weight
Is the intolerable pain I flee

The answer cannot lie in murder made easy
In fuelling guilt, complicity and dread
It lies in the courage to create a kinder world
In which no one would choose to be dead

Happily, I am not dead yet
I have lived to see another spring
I will use every precious moment I have left
This welcome change to bring

2006

Get It Right

When pondering what to call me
When trying to pick from possible descriptions
When noticing unusual features
And diminutive proportions
Let me inform you of a little known fact -
I am not a dwarf
I am not a midget

I am a cherub.

(A cherub is a cross between a large baby and a small angel)

2011

Birds for Life

The graceful avocet
The awesome albatross
The wheeling, shrieking kittiwakes
The tiny jenny wren
Seem to me beyond beauty
Filling the skies with life

To protect the smallest of them
We must protect their food

To protect their food
We must protect their plants

To protect their plants
We must protect their lands

To protect their lands
We must protect their peoples

To protect their peoples
We must give up greed
To protect our souls
Which sometimes we remember
Whilst watching the graceful avocet
The awesome albatross
The wheeling shrieking kittiwakes
Or the tiny jenny wren.

The Small Pleasures

Wind sending a rustling wave
Through the glowing late summer leaves
A mother grebe dipping and surfacing
Three stripy chicks disappearing
Beneath expanding circles of light
Re appearing downstream with a cheeky pop
A water vole shyly hurrying from delighted sight
Back to the safety of the homely rushes
A quick glimpse of a stone chat
Then two, then three
Singing on a wire fence
Before darting out of range of the scope
The strangers kindly adjust to my curious eye
A water snake gliding under the bridge
Slightly pre-historic, like the toad
Pretending to be a stone, until it moved
To gasps of passers by

The taste of a meal shared by two hungry explorers
Whilst the sunlit mud flats
Of the estuarine sea flooded with the intide
Intense pastel blues and pinks changing
By the minute
Into inky waters decorated
By glistening moonlit ripples
And twinkling shore line lights
Together we soaked up as much joy as possible
From these small and priceless pleasures

2009

They Lift Us Up

A friend clears a space for you to sit next to her on
your first day at school.
Shares an apple and a giggle and a packet of crisps
Says "See you tomorrow" as you rush back home
A lifeline from which to face the overwhelming
newness,
The terror of exclusion she has dulled into a faint
tremor.

A friend cheers for you as you prepare for the Date
Helps you decorate your face, tie up your hair, choose
your outfit
Even though the object of your desire
Whose invitation has set your heart racing,
Fantasies flowing,
Made all else pale into insignificance
Including her
Was in truth the object of her desire
Her dream crushed by your success, still
She is happy for you.

A friend gets out the board games he has brought
Draws his chair up to your bed
Declares that he is much happier
To play with you while your broken leg heals
Than join the other boys on the football pitch
Even though you know he is lying

A friend cannot wait to share with you
Their new kite, Barbie set, CD, Motorbike, 30"flat screen TV,
Read you their latest poem, sing you their new song,
Show you their latest photos,
Discuss with you their new thoughts
None seeming quite real until you have been witness to them

A friend gets up early, leaving her warm bed
On the one morning she has a chance to sleep in
To work your shift
Because you asked

A friend invites you to share an adventure
Travelling and exploring
Talking and laughing
Taking exciting risks because neither of you are alone
Building a bank of shared memories
To take out and re-visit in later days
When time and age have corralled you both
Into safer pastures

A friend notices that the love you feel
Has been temporarily submerged by the sleepless nights
The routine turned upside down
The loss of freedom
The one-way demand for attention
Listening to tears you were never allowed on your own behalf
He gently takes the crying baby from your arms
And lets you rest

A friend remembers your twenty fifth appointment
At the dreary hospital clinic
Driving you in and chatting by your side
As you wait in pain and dread for the next
Pronouncement on your demise

Our friends make life as it is bearable.
They are precious beyond measure.
But an Ally is even more than this.
They are not content for us to settle
In predetermined layers of worthiness
But lift us up
So we can see and fight and grow

An Ally asks what is has been like being us
Wants details
Allows the tears and the anger to surface
To dissipate rather than poison us from inside

An Ally treats us with respect

Especially when the dustbin lid of oppression

Presses down on our heads

Hiding the sky and forcing us to look down

When we feel as worthless as a spat out tasteless

piece of chewing gum

Blotching the pavement beneath our feet

An Ally says it is an honour to know us

When the bureaucrats and lackeys

Wear us down so that the millionth phone call we

need to make

For our survival

Threatens to unhinge our slender grip on sanity and

reason

An Ally will take the receiver and have the argument

on our behalf

An Ally may keep silent when their
Superior knowledge and experience would
Serve to stop us discovering our own thoughts
Instead wash our dishes so we have time to ponder
The challenging question she asked
When we begged for her advice
An Ally joins us on the barricades
Diverts resources in our direction
Furnishes us with information
Finds platforms for our voices to be heard
Uses their skills and influence to set us free

They may, or may not, giggle with us behind the
teachers back
Share our toys or our holidays
Sit by our sides when we are ill
Do the work we cannot manage
But they make
All real social change possible

The Rehabilitation Ward

Though I am but a short-stay bystander
Hooked up to my medicinal drip
I cannot help but be drawn into the drama
Of the rehabilitation ward

Twelve women thrown together
Bound by a common thread of suffering
Creating a personal world
In each numbered bed-space
Bringing life to the identical fixtures
Marked off by the curtained walls,
Privately closed or welcomely opened
A shocking-pink duvet here
A crochet blanket there
Books, bags, biscuits spread out,
Slippers under the bed
Trappings from home to bring comforting
memories
A shield from the insecure newness
Of the rehabilitation ward

Strangers at first they may be
But how rapidly the bonds are formed
When broken bodies and tired spirits
Cry out their universal language of pain!

The professionals offer a tough-love programme
Requiring courage, effort and grit
Their considerable skills and state-of-the-art resources
Backed up by devoted nursing
Are of little help
Without the heroic spirit
Of all their patients
Grasping the gold-dust opportunity
Feeling the pain
Pushing the boundaries of fear
Turning to each other
To cheer the small steps of progress
Sharing personal stories late in the evening
Shattering their isolation

An oasis of empathy
On the rehabilitation ward
It becomes apparent
That for many
Their present day injuries
Are a mere indication
Of a lifetime of struggle

Past anger, loss and disappointment
Once stored like poison
In joints and muscles
Released by the challenging
Stretches and movements
Rising up into consciousness
Find precious attention
Long held in tears
Shed at last
On a soft dressing-gowned shoulder
On the rehabilitation ward

The three weeks are over
Some leaving behind
Sticks and braces
Bowed bodies standing taller
Pain triumphantly driven
From centre stage
To the margins of their lives
Some taking with them
The restored ability
To laugh, they said.
The Hellos so cautious
Turn to reluctant Goodbyes
E-mail exchanges, shy kisses, careful hugs
Twelve ordinary women
Thrown together
Found true healing
On the rehabilitation ward

2011

Be Nice to Children and Save the World

What if every child
Were loved and fed
Kept safe from harm
Respected and admired
Nurtured and believed in
As a priority in our troubled world

What if every child
Were free from criticism and humiliation
Hunger and neglect
Violence and exploitation
Allowed to cry and heal their pain
Parents supported, not blamed

What a world we would create

Humans unfolding as we should

Never doubting our innate worth

Able to think

Connected and hopeful

No longer compelled to replay our childhood hurts

On anyone weaker than us

Could it be that simple?

Shall we give it a try?

2011

Inviting the Thieves Back In

Sleepwalking into chaos
Voting with our fear
We seem to have switched our brains off
Inviting the thieves back in

Their journalists did their job it seems
Pulled off their massive con
"They can't be worse than Brown" we bleated
"Let the others in"

Elected millionaires now preaching
The gospel of their greed
Filling their bursting coffers
From the denial of our need

I was raised in an era of hope
Our freedom so bravely defended
By young men rich and poor
Backed by the women's army
The War won, collective pride
The valuing of life, a sense of one
Planned a new world based on ideals

Schools and hospitals free to all
Council Houses, milk for children
Equal opportunities, human rights
Social security – a safety net
We burned our bras and grew our hair
Ban the Bomb and Greenham Common
Anti Apartheid and Save the Whales
Our Unions, our voices
Brass bands and male voice choirs
Dylan, Baez and Seeger
We sang and marched towards the light

Our successes scared them
The statistics now reveal
Behind closed doors
The world's elites
Closed rank
Globalised, privatised,
De regulated the banks

Disempowered our trade unions
Triumphantly broke our strikes
Sneered at our struggles for justice
As 'political correctness' gone mad

Did we all miss the turning
On the road to a better life?
Get confused, forget our dreams
Settle for material sops?
Did we fall asleep at the driving wheel
Are we surprised we crashed?

Better wake up, climb out of the wreckage
Finish what we began.

2011